Bible First™

THEN SAID JESUS..., IF YE CONTINUE IN MY WORD,
THEN ARE YE MY DISCIPLES INDEED;

AND YE SHALL KNOW THE TRUTH,
AND THE TRUTH SHALL MAKE YOU FREE.

JOHN 8:31–32

Bible First – Volume 3: Lessons 7-10
Copyright © 2016 by Euro Team Outreach, Inc.

Authors: Joshua Steele, Kelsie Steele, Teresa Beal, and Nathan Day

www.getbiblefirst.com

All Scripture quotations are taken from the King James Bible.

Publication date: March 2016
ISBN Print: 978-1-944679-02-6
ISBN eBook: 978-1-944679-08-8
ISBN ePDF: 978-1-944679-14-9
Library of Congress Control Number: 2016931523

1. Genesis; 2. Creation; 3. The Fall; 4. Adam and Eve; 5. Jesus Christ; 6. Cain and Abel; 7. Noah's Ark; 8. The Flood
I. Steele, Joshua; Steele, Kelsie; Beal, Teresa; Day, Nathan
II. Bible First – Volume 3: Lessons 7-10

Bible First – Volume 3: Lessons 7-10 may be purchased at special quantity discounts. Resale opportunities are available for sales promotions, corporate programs, gifts, fund raising, book clubs, or educational purposes for churches, congregations, schools and universities. For more information contact Mel Cohen: mel@euroteamoutreach.org
1000 Pearl Road
Pleasantville, TN 37033
931-593-2484

Editors: Katelin Day, Jessie Beal
Cover design: Joshua Steele
Interior layout: Joshua Steele
Publishing Consultant: Mel Cohen of Inspired Authors Press LLC
www.inspiredauthorspress.com

Printed in the United States of America

Contents

Also available in this series:

Foreword

Bible First was born in response to a need. In 2004, a small group of independent missionaries came together in western Ukraine to form a ministry known as Euro Team Outreach. Our primary objective was to communicate the Gospel of Jesus Christ to the Ukrainian people. As we searched for ways to do that effectively, we decided to launch a distance-learning course with the stated goal of encouraging people to read the Bible. It was our belief then – and still is today – that the Scriptures themselves represent the single most powerful witness of Christ on earth. To engage a sinner in reading God's Word is to dramatically increase his chances of believing on Christ for salvation. "So then faith cometh by hearing, and hearing by the word of God." (Romans 10:17)

Not finding any existing materials that fit our needs, we decided to write our own course. Our editing team, as we came to call it, included myself and my wife Kelsie, Jessie and Teresa Beal, and Nathan and Katelin Day. Though writing an entire Bible course from scratch was an ambitious goal, our approach was pragmatic. Certain of us drafted new material, and when significant portions were completed, the whole group would convene for editing meetings. Month after month we wrote, edited, rewrote and refined our work, striving to present the message of the Bible in a clear and engaging fashion.

The first lessons were mailed out in 2006 to Ukrainian students who enrolled in response to paper invitations. Soon our list of registered students began to grow, and we found it difficult to produce new material quickly enough to meet the demand. Authoring original curriculum is no easy task, and our efforts were further complicated by the fact that each of us had other ministry responsibilities outside of lesson writing. Additionally, every lesson we finished had to be translated into Ukrainian. Once a translation was complete, Nathan and I would read every word both in Ukrainian and English, meticulously comparing each line and requesting corrections from our translator when needed.

Months stretched into years, and still we kept writing. Every time we produced a new lesson for the course, there were already dozens of students waiting for it. I must confess there were days when I wondered if this task we had undertaken would ever be completed! Yet despite my wavering faith, God blessed our work, and *Bible First* continued to grow. Each summer, we conducted literature campaigns, expanding our reach to new cities and villages across Ukraine.

In time, we discovered that the back-and-forth nature of distance-learning provided an excellent context to communicate the Gospel and introduce people to studying Scripture for themselves. It also opened the door to true discipleship as existing *Bible First* students began to invite their friends to sign up. I still remember how thrilled I was one day when, as I studied some of our enrollment statistics, I realized that over 40% of our students were enrolling via word-of-mouth invitations from existing students!

The twentieth and final lesson of *Bible First* was completed in May of 2014. Since that time, we have seen a steady stream of Ukrainians graduating from the course, and many have expressed interest in becoming *Bible First* coaches themselves.

Our *Bible First* story would not be complete without acknowledging the efforts of Denise Hutchison. Denise joined ETO in 2009, and has worked tirelessly sending and receiving lessons, answering letters, and packaging up various books and Bibles to mail to our Ukrainian students. Over the years, her diligence in maintaining the day-to-day operations of *Bible First* allowed our editing team the time needed to create and refine new material.

Today, *Bible First* in Ukraine reaches students in every one of the country's 24 oblasts. Ukrainians are studying the Scriptures in big cities and small villages, at home, at school, and even from prison. Now, with the publication of *Bible First* in English, people in the United States and around the world can read these lessons for themselves and use them as a platform to point others to the Lord.

Bible First was created to encourage you, dear reader, to search the Scriptures. God has written and preserved His Holy Word, the Bible, so that every individual could have the opportunity to know Him. As you read what we have written in these lessons, may you be moved to read what *He* has written in the Bible. In John 20:31, the Apostle John reminds us: "…these are written, that ye might believe that Jesus is the Christ, the Son of God; and that believing ye might have life through his name."

Joshua Steele
L'viv, Ukraine
February 2016

The ETO Family
From the left: Denise, Jessie, Teresa, Katelin, Nathan, Kelsie, Joshua and Patricia

Euro Team Outreach

www.euroteamoutreach.org

How to Become a Coach

Bible First was designed as a platform for evangelism. In addition to the lessons themselves, we have created a variety of training materials and downloadable resources intended to help you launch your own ministry using the *Bible First* program.

To learn more about how you can become a *Bible First* coach, please visit us online at:

www.getbiblefirst.com/training

Bible First™

The Fall

How to complete this lesson

1. Read the text of the lesson.

Be sure to jot down any comments or questions you have as you read. You'll want to keep your Bible handy to look up passages as you progress through the lesson.

2. Answer the questions.

You'll find these in the Q&A booklet that you received from your coach. Be sure to write legibly.

3. Mail in the Q&A booklet.

Contact information for your coach can be found on the back of the Q&A booklet. Send your completed Q&A booklet to your coach along with any other comments or questions that you have.

Lesson Overview

- Two Marvelous Trees
- The First Command
- The Deceiver
- The Fall of Man
- Temptation Defined

Introduction

The third chapter of Genesis is one of the saddest passages in the Bible. It records a terrible event in human history known to most simply as *The Fall* - that fateful day when our father Adam turned away from God and plunged humanity into bondage.

The broken existence of sin and depravity that we see today does not reflect God's initial design. God intended man for glory and righteousness. Tragically, man chose to leave the path of light for a destiny of darkness.

The consequences of what occurred in the Garden of Eden transformed the earth from a realm of innocence and wonder into a world cursed with evil and suffering. Man, who began as a glorious ruler over God's creation, would now be separated from his Maker.

> Preliminary Reading – Before beginning this portion of the lesson, please read **Genesis 3:1-6** in your Bible.

Two Marvelous Trees

God's account of the fall of man in Genesis 3 centers around two extraordinary trees located in the Garden of Eden. *"And out of the ground made the LORD God to grow every tree that is pleasant to the sight, and good for food; the tree of life also in the midst of the garden, and the tree of knowledge of good and evil."* (Genesis 2:9)

Perhaps few realize that thousands of year ago in the Garden of Eden, God created the first and only fountain of youth: the Tree of Life. This tree, when partaken of, would cause man's natural body to continue in a state of perpetual health and vigor. Adam and Eve were completely free to eat of its fruit without limitation. Day by day, the Tree of Life strengthened their bodies and prevented the natural process of aging.

Later, after Adam and Eve sinned, God cast them out of the Garden of Eden primarily to separate them from the Tree of Life. *"And the Lord God said…and now, lest [man] put forth his hand, and take also of the tree of life, and eat, and live for ever: Therefore the Lord God sent him forth from the garden of Eden…and he placed at the east of the garden of Eden cherubims, and a flaming sword which turned every way, to keep the way of the tree of life."* (Genesis 3:22-24) God was notably concerned with preventing sinful man from accessing this tree and its incredible life-giving power.

The Bible reveals that in the future, humans will again partake of the wonderful fruit of the Tree of Life as a means of healing and preservation. The Book of Revelation speaks prophetically of this tree, saying, *"In the midst of the street of it, and on either side of the river, was there the tree of life, which bare twelve manner of fruits, and yielded her fruit every month: and the leaves of the tree were for the healing of the nations." (Revelation 22:2)*

Playing a more prominent role in the drama of the Garden of Eden was the Tree of Knowledge of Good and Evil. Eating the fruit of this tree allowed a person to attain to one of God's most basic characteristics: the ability to distinguish between right and wrong. Because Adam and Eve possessed only child-like moral discernment, partaking of the tree and increasing their understanding instantaneously could seem ideal. This however was not God's intent. His desire was to strengthen His two children by degrees, teaching them to recognize and withstand evil. He commanded Adam in no uncertain terms, *"...But of the tree of the knowledge of good and evil, thou shalt not eat of it: for in the day that thou eatest thereof thou shalt surely die." (Genesis 2:17)*

The contrast between these two amazing trees is significant. While eating of the Tree of Life offered the promise of an eternal existence, God warned that eating of the Tree of Knowledge of Good and Evil would result in certain death.

Key Concept

God intended man for glory and righteousness.

The First Command

"And the LORD God commanded the man, saying, Of every tree of the garden thou mayest freely eat: But of the tree of the knowledge of good and evil, thou shalt not eat of it: for in the day that thou eatest thereof thou shalt surely die." (Genesis 2:16-17)

God's desire is that men would obey Him of their own free will, even though they possess the ability to choose otherwise. Rather than create robots who were programmed to do only what would please Him, He designed man to be a free moral agent, able to choose between good and evil. God receives maximum glory and pleasure from one who lives with the continual possibility of sin and yet consistently chooses righteousness.

Thus, in a world where no evil existed, no possibility of choice between two paths, God placed the Tree of Knowledge of Good and Evil in the very middle of the garden and forbade Adam and Eve to eat of it. This command was a starting point for instilling in them the moral fortitude to continually say no to sin and yes to righteousness. God did not create sin, but He deliberately introduced the potential for sinful choices, knowing that without such choice, true moral character could not develop.

God is the most capable and loving of fathers. He knew that Adam and Eve's understanding was limited and their moral resistance feeble. Thus, He exposed them to good and evil slowly. Much in the way that a parent trains a small child, God presented Adam and Eve a simple choice, backed by a clear warning. The Tree of Knowledge of Good and Evil was the first "no" in their garden playpen. Had they not sinned, God's long-term goal would have been to introduce greater levels of choice until

His children matured to full moral strength.

Despite their inexperience, God's first command to Adam and Eve was simple, and the consequences for disobedience were clear. They had the power to obey and, enjoying open fellowship with God Himself, they also had ample instruction and strength to resist temptation.

The Bible Says

"See, I have set before thee this day life and good, and death and evil; In that I command thee this day to love the LORD thy God, to walk in his ways, and to keep his commandments and his statutes and his judgments, that thou mayest live and multiply: … But if thine heart turn away, … ye shall surely perish,…" (Deuteronomy 30:15-18)

Key Concept

God receives maximum glory and pleasure from one who lives with the continual possibility of sin and yet consistently chooses righteousness.

The Deceiver

"Now the serpent was more subtil than any beast of the field which the LORD God had made..." (Genesis 3:1)

At the opening of Genesis 3, a new character emerges onto the scene: the serpent. The Bible specifically mentions the cunning of this reptile, and sets him apart from every other creature in the garden. He possessed the power of speech and the ability to reason intelligently, freely conversing on the level of human thought. He was also aware of God's dealings with Adam and Eve.

Good and Evil, No Greater Joy Ministries

The serpent was likely quite different in appearance from the snakes of today. He may have stood upright, or walked on fours, as it was not until later that he was condemned to slither on his belly. There is no indication that he was repulsive in appearance, and in fact he may have been quite beautiful.

While the Bible doesn't mention Satan by name in Genesis 3, later passages reveal a clear link between the activities of the serpent and Satan's aspiration to rend world control away from Adam and Eve. Whether Satan indwelt the serpent to accomplish his plans, or whether the serpent was knowingly in league with Satan, the Scriptures do not say. One thing is clear: Satan directly orchestrated the temptation of Eve and plotted to bring about the fall of mankind.

Key Concept

Satan directly orchestrated the temptation of Eve and plotted to bring about the fall of mankind.

Key Concept

Adam and Eve had the power to obey and ample instruction and strength to resist temptation.

The Bible Explored

Consider the following parallels between the serpent of Genesis 3 and Satan himself.

- *"And I will put enmity between thee and the woman, and between thy seed and her seed; <u>it shall bruise thy head</u>, and thou shalt bruise his heel." (Genesis 3:15)* God's curse on the serpent also prophesies future conflict between him and the seed of the woman, which is Christ. It is foretold that the serpent would bruise the heel of Christ (a non-lethal wound) but that Christ would in turn bruise the head of the serpent (a lethal wound).

- *"And the God of peace shall <u>bruise Satan</u> under your feet shortly. The grace of our Lord Jesus Christ be with you. Amen." (Romans 16:20)* These words of Paul are a direct reference to the prophecy of Genesis 3, and also confirm the Scripture's portrayal of Satan and the serpent as essentially synonymous.

- *"And the great dragon was cast out, <u>that old serpent</u>, called the Devil, and Satan, which deceiveth the whole world: he was cast out into the earth, and his angels were cast out with him." (Revelation 12:9)* Satan is referred to directly as the old serpent. This emphasizes not only his snake-like nature, but also his age. He is the old serpent, the one spoken of since ancient times when he first tempted Eve.

- *"And he laid hold on the dragon, <u>that old serpent</u>, which is the Devil, and Satan, and bound him a thousand years," (Revelation 20:2)* Yet another reference to Satan as the old serpent.

- *"And said, O <u>full of all subtilty</u> and all mischief, thou child of the devil, thou enemy of all righteousness, wilt thou not cease to pervert the right ways of the Lord?" (Acts 13:10)* Speaking to a sorcerer, Paul the Apostle calls him a child of the devil and characterizes him as *being full of all subtlety*. God used this same description of the serpent in Genesis 3.

- *"Ye <u>serpents</u>, ye generation of <u>vipers</u>, how can ye escape* *the damnation of hell?" (Matthew 23:33)* Jesus, who repeatedly labeled the scribes and Pharisees as Satan's children, here calls them *serpents* and the *generation of vipers*. He clearly accentuates the link between the devil and the serpent.

- *"He that committeth sin is of the devil; for the devil sinneth from the beginning. For this purpose the Son of God was manifested, that he might destroy the works of the devil." (1 John 3:8)* A life of sin indicates a position in Satan's family tree. To serve sin is to acknowledge the Old Serpent as father.

- *"Forasmuch then as the children are partakers of flesh and blood, he [Christ] also himself likewise took part of the same; that through death he might destroy him that had the power of death, that is, the devil;" (Hebrews 2:14)* Here too is found a reference to the fulfillment of Genesis 3:15. Christ died on the cross (bruised by the serpent) that He might destroy Satan completely (the prophesied bruising of the serpent's head).

Key Concept

To serve sin is to acknowledge the Old Serpent as father.

The Fall

"Now the serpent was more subtil than any beast of the field which the LORD God had made. And he said unto the woman, Yea, hath God said, Ye shall not eat of every tree of the garden? And the woman said unto the serpent, We may eat of the fruit of the trees of the garden: But of the fruit of the tree which is in the midst of the garden, God hath said, Ye shall not eat of it, neither shall ye touch it, lest ye die. And the serpent said unto the woman, Ye shall not surely die: For God doth know that in the day ye eat thereof, then your eyes shall be opened, and ye shall be as gods, knowing good and evil. And when the woman saw that the tree was good for food, and that it was pleasant to the eyes, and a tree to be desired to make one wise, she took of the fruit thereof, and did eat, and gave also unto her husband with her; and he did eat." (Genesis 3:1–6)

Satan was certainly not pleased to see the establishment of God's perfect creation. As the archenemy of God and all that is good and true, his response was an endeavor to pervert God's design for man. Having been cast down from his former position as the exalted cherub, Satan was all the more infuriated to witness the prosperity of man. Adam was the new favorite, the young king upon whom God poured His love and blessing. Seething with rage and jealousy, Satan devised a plan to attack Adam's glorious reign and sever humanity's perfect communion with its Creator.

Satan knew from experience that he could never win an open war against God or against those under God's protection, so he turned to the only strategy left to him: deception. Rather than confront Adam directly, the serpent's first step was to seduce the woman, Adam's God-given helper and the one dearest to his heart. He began by casting doubt on the Word of God, raising the question, *"Yea, hath God said, Ye shall not eat of every tree of the garden?"* This was a blatant challenge to God's clear command, *"But of the tree of the knowledge of good and evil, thou shalt not eat of it..."* Thus Satan's first utterance in Scripture shows opposition to the Word of God. Satan's objective was to draw Eve away by his own words of subtlety. By questioning the veracity of God's words, Satan diminished Eve's fear of the punishment that would result from her disobedience.

Good and Evil, No Greater Joy Ministries

The serpent's next step was to cast doubt on the goodness of God. By assuring Eve that she could be godlike, the serpent led her to reason that God was unjustly withholding something from her. *"Ye shall not surely die: For God doth know that in the day ye eat thereof, then your eyes shall be opened, and ye shall be as gods, knowing good and evil."* Feigning concern for her welfare, he was seeking to undermine God's plan for her. In fact, God was the loving Creator who had made provision for all her needs. Now, due to the serpent's influence, God became suspect in Eve's thinking. Through cunning and deception, Satan succeeded in destroying Eve's childlike confidence in her Heavenly Father.

Finally, the serpent completed his attack by tempting Eve with the prospect of higher spirituality. *"For God doth know that in the day ye eat thereof, then your eyes shall be opened, and ye shall be as gods, knowing good and evil."* Exploiting her natural desire for enlightenment, Satan suggested to Eve that the results of eating the forbidden fruit would be pleasant and profitable. In reality, he was well aware of the terrible truth that Eve failed to discern: sin always leads to death.

Deceived and ignorant of the disaster that lay ahead, Eve did the unthinkable, rejecting her Father in exchange for the empty promises of the devil. With one seemingly insignificant bite of food, Eve disobeyed God and became a sinner.

The Devil's Accomplice

With Eve firmly in his grasp, Satan moved on to the pursuit of his true objective: the fall of Adam. But this attack would be different from the temptation of Eve. This time, Satan had someone who could approach Adam as an insider. Though stained with sin, Eve was still largely naive, and she was well-positioned to act as Satan's proxy, wielding tremendous influence over her husband.

The serpent must have smiled with wicked satisfaction as he watched his plan unfold. *"...And [Eve] gave also unto her husband with her; and he did eat." (Genesis 3:6)* As Adam took his first bite of the forbidden fruit, he too became a sinner, ending innocency in the Garden of Eden, and opening the door to millennia of darkness and suffering.

The Bible Says

"...When [Satan] speaketh a lie, he speaketh of his own: for he is a liar, and the father of it." (John 8:44)

Key Concept

One of the primary methods Satan uses to deceive men is to cast doubt on the Word of God.

The Bible Explored

Scripture reveals that although Eve was deceived by the serpent, Adam was not. *"And Adam was not deceived, but the woman being deceived was in the transgression."* *(1 Timothy 2:14)* In this sense, Adam's sin was the more inexcusable since he acted with greater understanding.

This begs the question: why did Adam capitulate? When he ate the forbidden fruit, Adam knew that he was disobeying God's command, and he knew that his transgression would result in death. So how could he possibly make such a suicidal choice?

The Scriptures do not answer this question directly, but a clue is found in Satan's strategy of attack. Certainly Satan could have chosen to tempt Adam first, but instead he targeted Eve. Clearly, he felt that this route offered him the greatest chance of success. Eve could be deceived, and once her fate was sealed, Adam would be forced to choose between his God and his wife. Satan gambled that Adam would choose Eve, and his gamble paid off.

While it seems reasonable to assume that God would have provided a means of redemption for Eve had Adam acted righteously, the scenario never presented itself. Adam chose evil, and in so doing he plunged humanity into darkness.

Did you know?

God's plan for testing and training men did not end with the Garden of Eden. While Adam and Eve were the only humans ever to encounter the original Tree of Knowledge of Good and Evil, choices for right and wrong still abound, like modern-day "Trees of Knowledge of Good and Evil."

The Tree in the Garden of Eden presented Adam and Eve with the opportunity to make a choice. Today, each impulse to say a hurtful word, each newsstand selling pornography, each case wherein telling a lie is easier than telling the truth, represents a challenge, like the Tree of Knowledge of Good and Evil, whereby God tests the hearts of men and women. It does not take long for Him to see who loves sin, and who loves righteousness. Those who pass by "the fruit of the tree" become stronger in spirit, while those who stop to partake allow themselves to become enslaved by fleshly passions.

Temptation Defined

When God created Adam and Eve, He gave them bodies with inherent physical drives. These drives - such as hunger, thirst, and sexuality, to name a few - are natural impulses that stem from needs and appetites *within* the body, requiring fulfillment from *outside* the body. Just as God is the creator of our bodies, so He is the creator of our bodily drives. Furthermore, God has provided natural, righteous means for the fulfillment of every drive He created.

Today, we have exactly the same physical needs and appetites that Adam and Eve had in the Garden of Eden. When Satan tempted Eve, he did so by appealing to natural and God-given bodily drives. Eve felt hunger because God created her body to derive its energy from food. Eve was attracted to the prospect of higher knowledge because God created people to be curious. Satan leveraged these and other natural appetites in order to tempt Eve and draw her into sin.

According to the Bible, temptation occurs when a person faces an opportunity to fulfill a natural, God-given drive in an unnatural, ungodly way. *"But every man is tempted, when he is drawn away of his own lust, and enticed. Then when lust hath conceived, it bringeth forth sin: and sin, when it is finished, bringeth forth death."* *(James 1:14–15)* In this passage, the word lust refers to the physical needs and appetites that God has placed within all of us. The progression from desire to destruction is simple: Lust (physical desire) → Temptation → Sin → Death. This progression demonstrates a profound fact: temptation and sin are distinct. It is quite possible to experience *temptation* and refuse the *sin* it offers.

The Bible states that Jesus Christ, the sinless Son of God, was *"... in all points tempted like as we are, <u>yet without sin.</u>"* *(Hebrews 4:15)* Some might wonder, "If Christ was sinless, how could He be tempted?" The answer is simple: because Christ had a physical body, just like Adam and Eve. In fact, we have a detailed account

of Christ's temptation experience in Matthew 4, which
demonstrates that Satan ap-
pealed to the physical desires
of Jesus' body in order to
tempt Him. After forty days
of fasting, Jesus was very
hungry. Satan suggested that
Jesus gratify His hunger in a
way that violated God's plan,
and Jesus rightly refused to
yield to his temptation.

God is the architect of all nature. To act in harmony with God's
design is to act naturally. To violate God's design is to go against
nature. Just as an auto-manufacturer builds his cars with an intended use in mind, so God made our bodies to be used in certain ways. And just as a driver is free to respect or violate the
manufacturer's design for his vehicle, so we are free to respect or
violate God's design for our bodies.

Often, people try to justify their sin by claiming that sinful behavior comes naturally. Such claims arise from a failure to distinguish between physical desire and moral choice. For example,
as we have already demonstrated, it is natural to feel hunger.
However, the bodily mechanisms which trigger the sensation of
hunger have no moral compass. Your body will feel satisfied if
you choose to eat food that belongs to you, but it will feel equally
satisfied if you choose to steal someone else's food. The moral as-
pect of your behavior has little to do with your natural impulses
and everything to do with your willingness - or lack thereof - to
obey God.

The physical bodies God has given us are beautiful, powerful
creations, endowed with a broad range of capabilities. We are
the stewards of our bodies, and God has given us the freedom to
use them as we will. We sit in the driver's seat, so to speak, and
it is our moral obligation to drive safely. If we use our bodies in

congruence with God's design, then we glorify Him. But if we use them unnaturally, let us remember who is to blame. When cars are driven recklessly, the fault lies not with the car, and not with its manufacturer, but with the driver.

"Lo, this only have I found, that God hath made man upright; but they have sought out many inventions." (Ecclesiastes 7:29)

Key Concept

Temptation occurs when a person faces an opportunity to fulfill a natural, God-given drive in an unnatural, ungodly way.

The Bible Says

"But every man is tempted, when he is drawn away of his own lust, and enticed. Then when lust hath conceived, it bringeth forth sin: and sin, when it is finished, bringeth forth death." (James 1:14–15)

The Bible Says

"The fear of the LORD is the beginning of wisdom: And the knowledge of the holy is understanding." (Proverbs 9:10)

Conclusion

The question has often been asked, "If God is sovereign, why did He allow mankind to fall into sin?" The answer is that God wanted a family of individuals who, like Himself, had the power of free choice. Certainly He could have created a race of robots, but moral character cannot be scripted. God desires fellowship with people who choose good voluntarily, even when faced with daily opportunities to choose evil.

Our Creator knew in advance that Adam and Eve would commit sin, and He prepared a plan for their redemption. In the New Testament, the Apostle Peter reveals that *"...[Christ] verily was <u>foreordained before the foundation of the world</u>, but was manifest in these last times for you," (1 Peter 1:20)* Although His coming did not occur until many years after the fall, Jesus Christ was set apart by God to become the Savior of humanity even before the earth was created.

Good and Evil, No Greater Joy Ministries

Today, our world remains separated from God because of what happened in the Garden of Eden. We live on a planet that has corporately rejected its Maker, and is therefore cursed to an existence of suffering and turmoil. Yet there is great comfort in the knowledge that God remains the Just Judge of all the universe. We are reminded in Scripture that God's wisdom is infinite, and His decisions are often beyond our ability to comprehend. *"O the depth of the riches both of the wisdom and knowledge of God! how unsearchable are his judgments, and his ways past finding out! For who hath known the mind of the Lord? or who hath been his coun-seller?" (Romans 11:33–34)* One thing God has made abundantly clear: His goodness and His love for each individual that He has created. We are not called to understand all His ways, but to trust Him, knowing that the God who formed the heavens is able to redeem every soul who turns to Him for salvation.

"Therefore as by the offence of one judgment came upon all men to condemnation; even so by the righteousness of one the free gift came upon all men unto justification of life." (Romans 5:18)

Notes

_____

_____

_____

_____

_____

_____

_____

_____

_____

_____

_____

_____

_____

_____

_____

_____

_____

_____

_____

_____

_____

_____

_____

Before continuing, please answer all the questions provided in the Q&A Booklet for this lesson. If you do not have a **Q&A Booklet** for this lesson, please contact your coach.

Bible First ™

The Curse and the
Promised Deliverer

How to complete this lesson

1. Read the text of the lesson.

Be sure to jot down any comments or questions you have as you read. You'll want to keep your Bible handy to look up passages as you progress through the lesson.

2. Answer the questions.

You'll find these in the Q&A booklet that you received from your coach. Be sure to write legibly.

3. Mail in the Q&A booklet.

Contact information for your coach can be found on the back of the Q&A booklet. Send your completed Q&A booklet to your coach along with any other comments or questions that you have.

Lesson Overview

- Adam's Choice to Sin
- Fear and Pride Enter the Garden
- The Curse
- God's Promised Deliverer

Introduction

"...In the day that thou eatest thereof thou shalt surely die." *(Genesis 2:17)* These chilling words must have echoed in the minds of Adam and Eve as they frantically searched for somewhere to hide in the Garden of Eden. This place which had once been their paradise home now seemed haunted with fear and dread. Only the day before they had walked with God in peace, enjoying His presence like children with their father. Now, as their world collapsed around them, they fled in shame, fearing that each moment might be their last.

God's warnings are never in vain. He does not bluff. Just as God promised, the entrance of sin into the Garden of Eden was followed by the curse of death. Tragically, the reach of that curse extended far beyond what Adam could have imagined, touching every one of his descendants. *"Wherefore, as by one man sin entered into the world, and death by sin; and so death passed upon all men, for that all have sinned:"* *(Romans 5:12)*

Despite Adam's failure, hope remained. The Scriptures reveal that the very principle which caused the sin of one man to ruin the lives of many, would later become the basis upon which the righteousness of One Man would redeem the world. *"...For if through the offence of one many be dead, much more the grace of God, and the gift by grace, which is by one man, Jesus Christ, hath abounded unto many."* *(Romans 5:15)*

Preliminary Reading – Before beginning this portion of the lesson, please read **Genesis 3:7-24** in your Bible.

Righteousness vs. Wickedness

All that God created was good. God Himself is righteous, and the Bible declares that He made man to be righteous also. *"Lo, this only have I found, that God hath made man upright..." (Ecclesiastes 7:29)* But evil was already present in God's beautiful world when Adam was placed in the Garden. Satan was allowed access to the Garden of Eden, no doubt as a test of Adam's loyalty to God. The day came when Adam faced a choice between righteousness and wickedness; between his loving Father and Satan.

The Steward of a Kingdom

When God placed Adam in the Garden, He made him a king. *"And God blessed them, and God said unto them, Be fruitful, and multiply, and replenish the earth, and subdue it: and <u>have dominion over the fish of the sea, and over the fowl of the air, and over every living thing that moveth upon the earth.</u>" (Genesis 1:28)* Adam was not a tenant, but a ruler who was given power and dominion over all that God had created. *"Thou madest [man] a little lower than the angels; thou crownedst him with glory and honour, and didst set him over the works of thy hands: Thou hast put all things in subjection under his feet..." (Hebrews 2:7–8)* As king, Adam was free to chart the course of his kingdom. His decisions would determine whether those under his reign would flourish in prosperity or wither in depravity.

God honored Adam's prerogative to choose between good and evil. Though certainly capable of intervention, God stood back and allowed Adam to exercise his independence. Today, each member of the human race retains that same freedom of choice. God speaks to individuals through His Word; He warns, He exhorts, and He persuades. But in the end, each person must make his decision, as Adam did, to follow God or to follow Satan.

Key Concept

All men have a free will to choose either good or evil.

Fear and Pride enter the Garden of Eden

Sin always brings consequences. The Bible says in Numbers 32:23 *"...be sure your sin will find you out."* Consequences may come quickly or they may be delayed, but they always come.

The first result of Adam and Eve's disobedience was the discovery of their nakedness. They turned from being God-conscious to being self-conscious. In an effort to hide their nakedness, Adam and Eve *"sewed fig leaves together, and made themselves aprons."* In their humiliation and guilt, they turned to the mere material protection of surrounding objects to cover their sinfulness. This is the first record we have of man attempting to remedy sin by his own efforts. Similarly, people today often rely on good works in an attempt to appease their guilty conscience.

Later that day, God came for His customary visit with Adam and Eve. But this time, they hid from Him, revealing a further consequence of Adam's sin - fear. *"And they heard the voice of the LORD God walking in the garden in the cool of the day: and Adam and his wife hid themselves from the presence of the LORD God amongst the trees of the garden."* (Genesis 3:8)

Key Concept

To hide from God is folly. It is always better to flee *to* God, than to flee *from* God.

The Bible Says

"He that covereth his sins shall not prosper: But whoso confesseth and forsaketh them shall have mercy." (Proverbs 28:13)

"And the LORD God called unto Adam, and said unto him, Where art thou?" (Genesis 3:9) God was not ignorant of his hiding place but sought rather to provide Adam an opportunity to repent of his own volition. Adam answered God, *"I heard thy voice in the garden, and I was afraid, because I was naked; and I hid myself."* God wisely answered this statement with another question, giving Adam further occasion to confess his transgression: *"Who told thee that thou wast naked? Hast thou eaten of the tree, whereof I commanded thee that thou shouldest not eat?"*

At this point, Adam could have repented. He could have cried out to God for mercy and forgiveness. It is not unreasonable to surmise that God would have forgiven Him and found a way to pay for his sin. But instead of repenting, Adam demonstrated another of sin's awful effects: pride. Pride is an abomination, the very sin for which Lucifer was cast out of heaven.

Adam's pride quickly displaced his love for Eve, and he turned against her, hoping to justify himself. He said to God, *"The woman whom thou gavest to be with me, she gave me of the tree, and I did eat."* Notice whom Adam blamed for his sin: *"The woman whom thou gavest..."* In other words, Adam implied that God was ultimately at fault for having created Eve in the first place.

This pattern of self-justification continued with Eve. She passed the blame to the serpent, claiming correctly that she had been deceived by him. The serpent, for his part, had no one to whom he could pass blame, nor did he try. He is the old enemy of God, and knew full well what to expect. His goal was not to deliver himself, but to cause the condemnation of Adam, his rival.

Thus Adam began a pattern of behavior that continues to permeate society today. Adam blamed his wife; Eve blamed the serpent. And ever since, we, the human race, have been trying to shift the blame from ourselves to anything or anyone else: the companions whom God has given us, the circumstances in which God has placed us, our parents who unfairly raised us, the peculiar temperament and disposition with which God has endowed us. But blaming others utterly fails to excuse sin. Even Adam and Eve recognized this in the end. Although they began with excuses, they were ultimately compelled to conclude with an admission of their guilt. When God pronounced sentence upon them, they did not argue, but silently accepted His ruling.

Key Concept

Blaming others utterly fails to excuse sin.

The Bible Says

"God resisteth the proud, but giveth grace unto the humble." (James 4:6)

The Curse

Beginning with the serpent, God justly pronounced judgment on each of the three offenders. It made no difference that two of them were His children. God is the Just and Holy Judge of the universe, and He cannot ignore sin. *"For there is no respect of persons with God." (Romans 2:11)*

God pronounced two judgments on the serpent. First, he was sentenced to crawl on his belly. Prior to being cursed, the serpent most likely stood upright. It was not until this point that he began to slither on his stomach. Secondly, the serpent was condemned to eat dust all the days of his life. In Scripture, the concept of licking the dust is referred to three other times and always typifies abject humiliation and disgrace. (See Psalm 72:9, Isaiah 49:23, Micah 7:17)

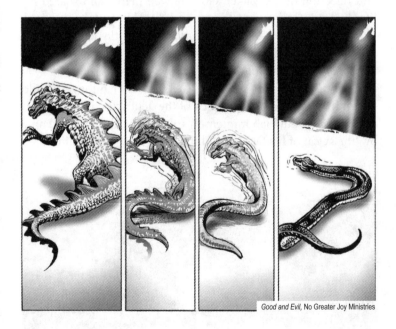

Good and Evil, No Greater Joy Ministries

God then addressed Eve's transgression. She was told that her sorrow would be greatly multiplied in bringing forth children. From that day on, the history of childbirth has been a striking fulfillment of the penalty pronounced upon Eve.

Furthermore, God made a statement to Eve about the nature of her relationship to Adam. God said that Eve's desire would be toward her husband and that he would rule over her. Submission to the man was not a curse in itself; it was a key part of God's original design for the woman. From the moment of her creation, Eve was given to Adam as his helper. She had the joy of being a beloved companion to a sinless husband. Now she would be ruled over by a fallen man, who no longer fully deserved the respect she would have to give him.

Finally, God turned to Adam. Before Him stood the one He loved, His creation, companion and friend, His son. God was now obliged to judge him for his wickedness. But even in this dark moment, God did not curse Adam. In spite of Adam's pride and rejection of his Maker, God showed mercy and spared his life. Instead, God cursed the ground. *"And unto Adam he said, Because thou hast hearkened unto the voice of thy wife, and hast eaten of the tree, of which I commanded thee, saying, Thou shalt not eat of it: cursed is the ground for thy sake; in sorrow shalt thou eat of it all the days of thy life;" (Genesis 3:17)* No longer would Adam freely and effortlessly pick of the delicacies of the Garden of Eden. He would labor intensely to produce his food, and only by "the sweat of his face" would the earth now yield to him.

After this, God foretold Adam's eventual death, and then drove both Adam and Eve out of the Garden of Eden. Cherubim were placed in the Garden to guard it from intruders. A flaming sword with power to swivel and rotate in any direction was placed at the entrance of the Garden so that no one could enter and eat of the Tree of Life again.

Sin had entered the world, and with it death. No longer could men eat of the healing fruit of the Garden of Eden. No longer could they enjoy fellowship with God. No longer could they see His face. Humanity had turned its back on God, and God withdrew.

Since that day, every man and woman born on this planet has chosen to sin as Adam did. And thus we see the truth of Romans 5:12 fulfilled: *"Wherefore, as by <u>one man</u> sin entered into the world, and death by sin; and so <u>death passed upon all men</u>, for that <u>all have sinned</u>:"*

The Bible Says

"If thou sayest, Behold, we knew it not; doth not he that pondereth the heart consider it? and he that keepeth thy soul, doth not he know it? and shall not he render to every man according to his works?" (Proverbs 24:12)

Adam's Choice Defined

In order to properly understand the curse which came upon our planet, it is also necessary to understand the nature of Adam's choice. Some have wondered, "Why did God respond with such severity? Did Adam really have to die for eating fruit? Couldn't God have given Adam a second chance?" Such questions demonstrate a lack of understanding as to the gravity of sin. Sin is like a deadly virus, which begins as a tiny, seemingly insignificant organism. Given the opportunity, it will multiply into a plague, threatening not only the life of its host, but the lives of all those to whom it spreads.

To characterize Adam's actions merely as the consumption of fruit is to miss the point entirely. Adam chose to disobey God. In rebellion to his Creator, he knowingly stepped off the path of light and gave his crown to the devil.

The Bible Says

"For there is no respect of persons with God." (Romans 2:11)

The Bible Says

"For the wages of sin is death…" (Romans 6:23)

Did you know?

Snakes deliberately lick and eat dust. There is an organ in the roof of a snake's mouth called the Jacobson's organ. This organ operates in conjunction with the nose, enhancing the snake's ability to smell. The snake's  darting, forked tongue samples bits of dust by picking them up on the points of the fork, which it then presents to its matching pair of sensory organs inside its mouth. Once it has analyzed them in this way, the tongue must be cleaned so the process can be repeated immediately. Therefore, serpents really do lick dust and eat it just as it says in Isaiah 65:25, *"The dust shall be the serpent's meat."*

Key Concept

God is the Just and Holy Judge of the universe, and He cannot ignore sin.

Why didn't Adam die?

It is commonly wondered why Adam and Eve did not die the same day they ate of the forbidden fruit. After all, God was very specific in His original warning to them: *"But of the tree of the knowledge of good and evil, thou shalt not eat of it: <u>for in the day that thou eatest thereof</u> thou shalt surely die." (Genesis 2:17)* There is no doubt that Adam understood this warning clearly, for when God sought him later, Adam hid.

Good and Evil, No Greater Joy Ministries

So why didn't Adam die that day? Why did he in fact live for several hundred more years? The Bible does not say specifically why God spared Adam's life, but upon closer examination of the passage, we see that there was indeed a death which occurred that very day in the Garden of Eden. *"Unto Adam also and to his wife did the LORD God make coats of skins, and clothed them." (Genesis 3:21)* God killed animals in order to make coverings for Adam and Eve.

Later Adam's son, Abel, brought his sheep to the Lord as a sacrifice, and God was pleased with the offering. Where did Abel learn this practice? It may be that God made the first blood sacrifice in history when He killed two animals that day in the Garden instead of killing Adam and Eve.

One thing is certain: God showed great mercy to Adam and Eve. And God's mercy was not limited merely to the delay of their physical deaths. In the remainder of Genesis 3, God revealed to Adam and Eve His magnificent plan to bring full redemption to mankind.

God's Promised Deliverer

When God pronounced His curse on the serpent He said, *"Because thou hast done this, thou art cursed above all cattle... And I will put enmity between thee and the woman, and between thy seed and her seed; it shall bruise thy head, and thou shalt bruise his heel."*

Good and Evil, No Greater Joy Ministries

(Genesis 3:14-15) In other words, God said that the seed (offspring) of the serpent would fight against the seed of the woman. Moreover, God prophesied that the woman's seed would destroy the serpent's seed. But why did God emphasize the seed of the *woman*?

In the Old Testament, the prophet Isaiah makes this amazing statement: *"Therefore the Lord himself shall give you a sign; Be-hold, a virgin shall conceive, and bear a son, and shall call his name Immanuel."* *(Isaiah 7:14)* For a woman to conceive without a man is a biological impossibility. Yet God prophesied in Genesis 3 and also in Isaiah 7 that it would happen. There in the Garden of Eden, in the midst of the *first* man's utter failure, God announced the coming of a *second* Man who would be born of a virgin and who would destroy the devil.

Scripture contains literally hundreds of prophecies of the coming Deliverer. At last, in Matthew 1:20-25, the Deliverer's identity is fully revealed: *"...the angel of the Lord appeared unto [Joseph] in a dream, saying, Joseph, thou son of David, fear not to take unto thee Mary thy wife: for that which is conceived in her is of the Holy Ghost. And she shall bring forth a son, and thou shalt call his name JESUS: for he shall save his people from their sins. Now all this was done, that it might be fulfilled which was spoken of the Lord by the prophet [Isaiah], saying, Behold, a virgin shall be with*

*child, and shall bring forth a son, and they shall call his name Em-
manuel, which being interpreted is, God with us. Then Joseph being raised from sleep did as the angel of the Lord had bidden him,
and took unto him his wife: And knew her not till she had brought
forth her firstborn son: and he called his name JESUS."*

"...and thou shalt call his name **JESUS** for he shall save his people from their sins."

The Deliverer whom God promised to Adam and Eve that sad
day in the Garden was none other than our Savior, the Lord Jesus Christ. Over time, God continued to reveal more of His plan,
reminding His people that one day, the Deliverer would come to
save them from their sins.

Did you know?

The Old Testament contains a myriad of prophesies about the Promised Deliverer. Some are vague, but some are very clear and precise. There are different opinions on their exact number, but the general agreement is that there are at least 300. The mathematician and scientist Peter Stoner[1] once estimated the chances of one person fulfilling the Scripture's predictions. For example, the odds of the Promised Deliverer being born in Bethlehem, as prophesied in Micah 5:2, are one in 300,000 (or 3×10^5). When 7 more prophesies are added to the equation, the likelihood of one person fulfilling all of them drops to one in 10^{17} (a one followed by 17 zeros)! To grasp the size of this number, imagine counting from 1 to 10^{17} at the rate of one number per second. It would take over 3 billion years to reach 10^{17}! Despite the incredible odds, God fulfilled all of these prophesies through his Son, the Lord Jesus Christ.

The Bible Says

"The first man is of the earth, earthy: the second man is the Lord from heaven." (1 Corinthians 15:47)

---

1. "The Christ of Prophecy." http://www.sciencespeaks.net/

Conclusion

When Adam began his downward spiral into sin and darkness, he acted alone. No one forced his hand. He was tempted, he was influenced by evil outside of his control, and he was even moved by love for his wife. But in the end, Adam made his own decision.

The same is true of us today. Although we live in a world filled with evil and wickedness, ruled by Satan himself, we retain our free will to choose. Every person who sins against God does so of his own volition. Men are born on a planet that is cursed because of Adam's transgression, but corruption is a curse that they bring upon themselves through their own choice to sin.

The Bible says, *"Know ye not, that to whom ye yield yourselves servants to obey, his servants ye are to whom ye obey; whether of sin unto death, or of obedience unto righteousness?"* (Romans 6:16) Sin makes slaves of us all, and slaves can only be freed if someone pays the price of their redemption. Jesus Christ came into the world to do just that. God sent Him to be our Redeemer, our Deliverer. God desires that all men would be reconciled to Him and washed from their sins in the blood of the Lord Jesus.

Key Concept

Separation from God is universal, based on the sin of Adam, but guilt is personal, based on the choices of the individual.

Notes

_____

_____

_____

_____

_____

_____

_____

_____

_____

_____

_____

_____

_____

_____

_____

_____

_____

_____

_____

_____

_____

_____

_____

_____

_____

_____

_____

Notes

_____

_____

_____

_____

_____

_____

_____

_____

_____

_____

_____

_____

_____

_____

_____

_____

_____

_____

_____

_____

_____

_____

_____

Before continuing, please answer all the questions provided in the Q&A Booklet for this lesson. If you do not have a Q&A Booklet for this lesson, please contact your coach.

Bible First™

Cain and Abel

How to complete this lesson

1. Read the text of the lesson.

Be sure to jot down any comments or questions you have as you read. You'll want to keep your Bible handy to look up passages as you progress through the lesson.

2. Answer the questions.

You'll find these in the Q&A booklet that you received from your coach. Be sure to write legibly.

3. Mail in the Q&A booklet.

Contact information for your coach can be found on the back of the Q&A booklet. Send your completed Q&A booklet to your coach along with any other comments or questions that you have.

Introduction

Adam and Eve were now beginning their lives outside the Garden of Eden. Not only had they been cast out from the Garden, they had been separated from God Himself. These two were the only ones to ever enjoy physical, direct access to God's presence on the earth. Their children would not know this privilege, and would suffer from the same separation as Adam and Eve, even though they did not commit the initial sin against God.

What began with a seemingly simple act of disobedience in the Garden grew into a long, tragic line of evil. Small offenses led to bigger ones. Jealousy turned to hatred, and hatred eventually led to murder. The consequences of sin always extend far beyond the original transgression.

In order to deal with man's sin, God introduced the blood sacrifice. God intended that this practice be a reminder to men that one day, the Promised Deliverer would come and shed His own blood as a final atonement for sin. Finally, God began the careful preservation of a lineage from which this Promised Deliverer would come.

> Preliminary Reading – Before beginning this portion of the
> lesson, please read **Genesis 4:1-7** in your Bible.

A Man from the Lord

*"And Adam knew Eve his wife; and she conceived, and bare Cain,
and said, I have gotten a man from the LORD."* (Genesis 4:1) For
the first time in history, a man and woman came together, and a
new life was conceived. When the child was born, Adam and Eve
named him Cain. Today he is known as the first murderer in human history, but when he was born, Eve had a different thought.
Her declaration about her son is very interesting: *"I have gotten a
man from the LORD."* Eve was waiting for God's Promised Deliverer. She understood that this Deliverer would not miraculously
descend from the clouds or come up from the sea. He would be
born from the seed of a woman as God foretold in Genesis 3:15.
Could Cain be the One? Only time would tell, for in order to
deliver mankind from sin, this Deliverer must Himself be free
from sin.

Good and Evil, No Greater Joy Ministries

An Acceptable Sacrifice

Eve conceived again and gave birth to her second son, Abel. The Bible does not give us any details about Cain and Abel's childhood, but we can imagine that from an early age, Cain and Abel worked very hard. They lived without the benefit of modern machinery or technology, fashioning their own tools, doing everything by hand. Their parents must have taught them how to plant and harvest crops that were now essential for their sur-

Good and Evil, No Greater Joy Ministries

vival. They were instructed in how to raise animals and tend herds, protecting them from animals of prey. As they grew older, Cain and Abel likely chose their own occupations, specifically: *"...Abel was a keeper of sheep, but Cain was a tiller of the ground." (Genesis 4:2)*

No doubt Adam and Eve also carefully explained to Cain and Abel the details of the fall and the prophecy of the Promised Deliverer. In addition, Adam must have taught his sons the necessity of bringing sacrifices to the Lord. *"And in process of time it came to pass, that Cain brought of the fruit of the ground an offering unto the LORD. And Abel, he also brought of the firstlings of his flock and of the fat thereof..." (Genesis 4:3-4)* This practice of offering sacrifices would continue throughout the Scriptures as people came to the Lord seeking reconciliation and forgiveness.

It soon became evident that neither Cain nor Abel could be the Promised Deliverer. In order to save others from sin, the Deliverer must be free from sin Himself. If He were a sinner, He would have to die for His own sins and would thus be unable to bear the sins of others. By offering sacrifices, Cain and Abel acknowledged their own sinfulness and need for reconciliation with God.

Key Concept

In order to save others from sin, the Promised Deliverer must be free from sin Himself.

Not only do the Scriptures record Cain and Abel's offerings to the Lord, but also God's response to those offerings. *"...And the LORD had respect unto Abel and to his offering: But unto Cain and to his offering he had not respect. And Cain was very wroth, and his countenance fell." (Genesis 4:4-5)* The Bible records that both men brought offerings from their respective occupations. Abel brought a lamb from his flock, while Cain brought fruits and vegetables which he had grown. No doubt both Cain's produce and Abel's lamb had material value, yet God received Abel's offering and rejected Cain's. From a human standpoint, this rejection may seem unjust. Cain brought what he had; he gave beautiful produce, the result of many hours of hard labor and dedication. Why then did God reject his sacrifice but not Abel's?

Good and Evil, No Greater Joy Ministries

The Scriptures are very clear that the purpose of a sacrifice is not to present God with something of value, but rather to pay for sin. According to the Bible, there is only one thing that can pay for a person's sin: blood. In Leviticus 17:11 God says, *"For the life of the flesh is in the blood: and I have given it to you upon the altar to make an atonement for your souls: for it is the blood that maketh an atonement for the soul."*

Cain's offering was rejected because it was not a blood offering. His fruits and vegetables were not sufficient to atone for the soul. To atone means to reconcile two estranged parties by making compensation or amends for past offenses. When a man sins against God, that sin separates him from God. *"But your iniquities have separated between you and your God, and your sins have hid his face from you, that he will not hear."* (Isaiah 59:2) God cannot look upon sin, and without proper atonement, the sinner can never be restored to a place of fellowship and peace with his Creator. Material possessions can never atone for sin. Water cannot cleanse away sin. Even all our good works are completely insufficient to atone for sin. God rejects these things just as He rejected Cain's offering.

Key Concept

Only blood can pay for sin.

There are some who say, "I will come to God on my own terms. He will accept me as I am." This was also Cain's attitude. But God countered in Genesis 4:6-7: *"...Why art thou wroth? and why is thy countenance fallen? If thou doest well, shalt thou not be accepted? and if thou doest not well, sin lieth at the door..."* To be accepted of the Lord, one must do well. In other words, one must come on God's terms. To reject God's terms is to sin further against Him.

The Scriptures clearly teach that God demands blood sacrifice as the only acceptable payment for sin. Even the ministry of the Lord Jesus, which was full of good works, would have proven worthless in establishing our relationship with God had He not died on the cross in our place. He *"...went about doing good..."* (Acts 10:38) all of His life, but it is His death and the shedding of His blood that reconciles us to God.

Cain attempted to come to God bearing only his own good works instead of a blood sacrifice as God commanded. This embodies the false ground upon which Cain stood as an offerer and a worshiper. He openly rebelled against God and was rejected because of it.

When Abel brought his lamb to God, he shed its blood. The lamb was innocent, and its poured-out blood demonstrated that a sinless life had been given as a saving substitute for Abel's life. Because the lamb died on the altar, Abel would be spared. God accepted Abel's offering because it was a blood sacrifice according to His pattern.

The Bible Says

"For the life of the flesh is in the blood: and I have given it to you upon the altar to make an atonement for your souls: for it is the blood that maketh an atonement for the soul." (Leviticus 17:11)

Key Concept

To atone means to reconcile two estranged parties by making compensation or amends for past offenses.

Preliminary Reading – Before beginning this portion of the lesson, please read **Genesis 4:8-16** in your Bible.

The First Murder

After Cain's offering was rejected, God gave him a second chance, encouraging him to bring a blood sacrifice like Abel's. *"If thou doest well, shalt thou not be accepted?..."* *(Genesis 4:7)* Unfortunately, instead of following the example of his younger brother, Cain grew even more angry. He discarded God's statement that he would be ruler over his younger brother Abel. *"Unto thee shall be his desire, and thou shalt rule over him."* Cain's anger intensified until it culminated in a tragic and irreparable action. *"And Cain talked with Abel his brother: and it came to pass, when they were in the field, that Cain rose up against Abel his brother, and slew him."* *(Genesis 4:8)*

Did you know?

Leviticus 17:11 contains a wealth of scientific truth. Contrary to what this Scripture teaches, bloodletting was widely practiced in ancient and medieval medicine. A broad assortment of ailments was believed to result from the impurity or overabundance of blood in the body.

In 1620, William Harvey demonstrated the circulation of blood throughout the body. It was not until that time that the scientific community realized the crucial role that blood plays. Even then, the practice of bloodletting continued into the 19th century, despite what was written several thousand years ago in the Bible.

The Bible Explored

God has much to say in the Bible about murderers.

Those who murder follow their father, the devil. Jesus said to the Pharisees:

■ *"Ye are of your father the devil, and the lusts of your father ye will do. He was a murderer from the beginning..." (John 8:44)*

The punishment for murder is death. God says:

■ *"Whoso sheddeth man's blood, by man shall his blood be shed: for in the image of God made he man." (Genesis 9:6)*

■ *"Moreover ye shall take no satisfaction for the life of a murderer, which is guilty of death: but he shall be surely put to death." (Numbers 35:31)*

Good and Evil, No Greater Joy Ministries

God sees hatred as murder.

■ *"Whosoever hateth his brother is a murderer: and ye know that no murderer hath eternal life abiding in him." (1 John 3:15)*

The blood of a murderer's victim cries out to God for vengeance, and God hears this cry.

■ *"And [God] said, What hast thou done? the voice of thy brother's blood crieth unto me from the ground." (Genesis 4:10)*

God Shows Mercy to Cain

In the wake of Abel's murder, God's first course of action was to approach Cain. The Bible says that God sees and knows everything, and yet he did not begin his discourse by accusing Cain. Instead, by asking a simple question about Abel's whereabouts, God gave Cain the opportunity to confess his fault. *"And the LORD said unto Cain, Where is Abel thy brother? And he said, I know not: Am I my brother's keeper?" (Genesis 4:9)* Rather than admitting to Abel's murder, Cain replied with sarcasm and falsehood, as if to say, "How should I know? I'm not responsible for my brother. Go look for him yourself." The Lord then confronted Cain with his sin: *"And [God] said, What hast thou done? the voice of thy brother's blood crieth unto me from the ground." (Genesis 4:10)*

As noted previously, God demands death for murderers. However, Genesis 4 reveals that Cain did not die right away. In fact, the judgment God pronounced on him is quite similar to that which He pronounced on Adam. God said to Cain, *"And now art thou cursed from the earth, which hath opened her mouth to receive thy brother's blood from thy hand; When thou tillest the ground, it shall not henceforth yield unto thee her strength; a fugitive and a vagabond shalt thou be in the earth." (Genesis 4:11-12)*

Instead of grieving at the enormity of his sin, Cain complained about the severity of his judgment and said, *"...My punishment is greater than I can bear. Behold, thou hast driven me out this day from the face of the earth; and from thy face shall I be hid; and I shall be a fugitive and a vagabond in the earth; and it shall come to pass, that every one that findeth me shall slay me." (Genesis 4:13-14)*

One might expect that God would be very angry with Cain because he murdered his brother, Abel, showed no remorse, and refused to repent. But the response God gave Cain is astonishing! *"And the LORD said unto him, Therefore whosoever slayeth Cain, vengeance shall be taken on him sevenfold. And the LORD set a mark upon Cain, lest any finding him should kill him." (Genesis 4:15)* Not only did God spare Cain's life, but He also put a mark on his body to prevent any other person from killing him. Why did God show this kind of mercy to Cain, especially considering the fact that Cain showed no remorse? How could God be just and still withhold punishment for Cain's sin?

The truth is, God often waits before passing final judgment on sinners. His forbearance does not indicate that he approves of sin, nor that He is indifferent to it. Rather, God mercifully gives a sinner time to consider his error and repent. *"And thinkest thou this, O man, that judgest them which do such things, and doest the same, that thou shalt escape the judgment of God?* <u>*Or despisest thou the riches of his goodness and*</u>

Good and Evil, No Greater Joy Ministries

<u>*forbearance and longsuffering; not knowing that the goodness of God leadeth thee to repentance?*</u> *But after thy hardness and impenitent heart treasurest up unto thyself wrath against the day of wrath and revelation of the righteous judgment of God;" (Romans 2:3-5)* God's goodness and forbearance are intended to lead a sinner to repentance, but if he continues in his wickedness God will eventually destroy him.

Accordingly, God gave Cain opportunity to repent, but the Bible

Key Concept

God often waits to judge sinners in order to give them time to repent.

reveals that Cain rejected God's mercy. *"And Cain went out from the presence of the LORD, and dwelt in the land of Nod, on the east of Eden. And Cain knew his wife; and she conceived, and bare Enoch: and he builded a city, and called the name of the city, after the name of his son, Enoch." (Genesis 4:16-17)* Cain left the Lord's presence that day and never returned. One of the final statements in the Bible regarding Cain is in 1 John 3:12, *"Not as Cain, who was of that wicked one, and slew his brother. And wherefore slew he him? Because his own works were evil, and his brother's righteous."*

The Bible Says

"…As I live, saith the Lord GOD, I have no pleasure in the death of the wicked; but that the wicked turn from his way and live: turn ye, turn ye from your evil ways; for why will ye die…?" (Ezekiel 33:11)

Did you know?

The Bible states clearly that it is God's desire for all men to repent and be delivered from their sin. *"The Lord is not slack concerning his promise, as some men count slackness; but is longsuffering to us-ward, not willing that any should perish, but that all should come to repentance." (2 Peter 3:9)*

Preliminary Reading – Before beginning this portion of the lesson, please read **Genesis 4:17-26** in your Bible.

The Line of Seth

The final verses of Genesis 4 give the genealogy of Cain. Sadly, as Earth's population increased, so did its transgressions. One of Cain's descendants, Lamech, also committed murder. Just as Cain sought to justify himself after his sin, so Lamech made excuses for his actions in an attempt to avoid condemnation.

Not only was it now clear beyond all doubt that Cain could not be the Promised Deliverer, but his descendants proved themselves to be just as wicked as he was, following in his footsteps. In time, families became so corrupt that the children had no example of righteousness in their homes. The Bible gives an interesting description of this trend of evil, calling it "the way of Cain." *"But these speak evil of those things which they know not: but what they know naturally, as brute beasts, in those things they corrupt themselves. Woe unto them! for they have gone in the way of Cain..." (Jude 1:10-11)*

God intervened in man's sinful decline and began a new lineage on the earth. *"And Adam knew his wife again; and she bare a son, and called his name Seth: For God, said she, hath appointed me another seed instead of Abel, whom Cain slew." (Genesis 4:25)* Unlike his brother Cain, Seth followed the Lord and walked in righteousness. Furthermore, he trained his children to do so. *"And to Seth, to him also there was born a son; and he called his name Enos: then began men to call upon the name of the LORD." (Genesis 4:26)* To call on the name of the Lord is to acknowledge Him, to turn to Him for help, to believe His Word. Seth taught his family these things and led them in following God. Much later in Scripture, the Gospel of Luke tells us that God chose the lineage of Seth to bring the Promised Deliverer into the world. (See Luke 3:23-38)

Conclusion

The fourth chapter of Genesis provides significant insight into God's dealings with man. Of these dealings, one of the most important is the blood sacrifice. As the sacrifices of Cain and Abel demonstrate, blood had to be offered to cleanse away sin. Any sin, no matter how small, merits God's judgment. The Bible is clear that if a sinner is not reconciled to God, the end result is death.

- *"For the wages of sin is death..." (Romans 6:23)*
- *"Behold, all souls are mine;...the soul that sinneth, it shall die." (Ezekiel 18:4)*

The only possible means of delivering a sinner from the terrible condemnation awaiting him is to substitute the life of one who is innocent. Either the sinner must die, or another must die in his place. This is the meaning of sacrifice.

In this lesson, Abel made an animal sacrifice to atone for his sin, and God accepted it. However, the New Testament declares that *"...it is not possible that the blood of bulls and of goats should take away sins." (Hebrews 10:4)* If animal sacrifices cannot take away sin, why did God command them to be made? Why did He bless those like Abel, who offered them?

Good and Evil, No Greater Joy Ministries

When God ordained blood sacrifices, He had three main objectives in mind. The first objective was to give humanity a way to temporarily pay for their sin. Secondly, God wanted to teach them the meaning of atonement. Each time they sinned, they had to bring an innocent animal and kill it on an altar before the Lord. By offering sacrifices, they would be continually reminded that innocent blood was being shed as a covering for their sin. God's third objective in ordaining blood sacrifices was to prepare mankind for the coming of the Promised Deliverer, the Lord Jesus Christ. When Jesus came to earth thousands of years later, he was introduced by John the Baptist in a very interesting way:

"...Behold the Lamb of God, which taketh away the sin of the world." (John 1:29)

Good and Evil, No Greater Joy Ministries

The Bible says: *"Neither by the blood of goats and calves, but by [Christ's] own blood he entered in once into the holy place, having obtained eternal redemption for us. For if the blood of bulls and of goats, and the ashes of an heifer sprinkling the unclean, sanctifieth to the purifying of the flesh: How much more shall the blood of Christ, who through the eternal Spirit offered himself without spot to God, purge your conscience from dead works to serve the living God?" (Hebrews 9:12-14)*

Jesus came to offer His sinless life as the perfect and lasting sacrifice for us. The animal sacrifices of the Old Testament had to be offered daily, but Jesus died once and for all to save sinners. He then rose from the grave, having conquered forever the power of sin and death.

Key Concept

When God ordained blood sacrifices, He had three main objectives in mind:

1. To give humanity a means of temporarily paying for their sin.
2. To teach them the meaning of atonement.
3. To prepare mankind for the coming of the Promised Deliverer.

Notes

_____

_____

_____

_____

_____

_____

_____

_____

_____

_____

_____

_____

_____

_____

_____

_____

_____

_____

_____

_____

_____

_____

_____

_____

_____

_____

_____

_____

Before continuing, please answer all the questions provided in the Q&A Booklet for this lesson. If you do not have a **Q&A Booklet** for this lesson, please contact your coach.

Bible First™

Noah and the Great Flood

How to complete this lesson

1. Read the text of the lesson.

Be sure to jot down any comments or questions you have as you read. You'll want to keep your Bible handy to look up passages as you progress through the lesson.

2. Answer the questions.

You'll find these in the Q&A booklet that you received from your coach. Be sure to write legibly.

3. Mail in the Q&A booklet.

Contact information for your coach can be found on the back of the Q&A booklet. Send your completed Q&A booklet to your coach along with any other comments or questions that you have.

Lesson Overview

- The Righteous Judgment of God
- Noah, the Preacher of Righteousness
- The Great Flood
- The Tower of Babel
- God's Provision for Deliverance from Judgment

Introduction

As men multiplied on the earth, so did their transgressions against the Lord. By the time of Noah, the human race had so corrupted itself that, in the words of the Bible, "*...every imagination of the thoughts of [their] heart was only evil continually.*" *(Genesis 6:5)* The remainder of Genesis 6 describes God's response to this evil: the greatest cataclysmic event in the history of the world. However, this record is more than a narrative of judgment. It paints a picture of the vast mercy of God, extended to all who will come to Him in faith.

Preliminary Reading – Before beginning this portion of the lesson, please read **Genesis 5** in your Bible.

Genealogy of Adam

Genesis 5 recounts the genealogy of Adam, detailing his lineage from Creation through Noah and his sons. Of particular interest are the unusually long lifespans as recorded in this passage, often in excess of 900 years. In our day, when the average lifespan is around 70 years, many people find it hard to believe this record. However, given a different environment, it would be quite possible for the human body to live for longer periods of time.

Archeological findings testify that the climate on earth was once much different. In Antarctica, scientists have found fossils of various plants and animals that could only survive in a temperate environment, much different from Antarctica's year-round frigid temperatures of today. Evidence suggests that this change from a tropical climate to a dryer, cooler climate occurred directly after the flood. This would also explain the declining life spans found in Genesis 11. Noah himself lived to be 950, but his son, Shem, lived to be 600, and Noah's grandson, Arphaxad, only lived to be 438, less than half of Noah's lifespan. By the time of Abraham's birth at the close of Genesis chapter 11, a mere 292 years after the flood, man's average lifespan had dropped to around 200 years.

The Bible Says

"So teach us to number our days, that we may apply our hearts unto wisdom." (Psalm 90:12)

Did you know?

Scientists have proposed many theories regarding the prehistoric living conditions that once existed. Some suggest that there was a canopy of water in the atmosphere that protected the earth from the sun's harmful rays, while at the same time creating a greenhouse effect. This caused a milder, tropical climate throughout the entire earth, an atmosphere friendlier to living organisms. According to this theory, the canopy of water fell to earth during the great flood, resulting in the colder climate of today.

Others say that the earth's atmosphere once contained a slightly higher percentage of oxygen which made life possible for now-extinct animal species. These elevated oxygen levels may have also helped to prolong the life of man.

Preliminary Reading – Before beginning this portion of the lesson, please read **Genesis 6** in your Bible.

The Wickedness of Man

As time passed, people became exceedingly wicked. They cast aside the commands of the Lord and engaged in all manner of sin. Because of their wicked works, their hearts grew dark. *"...when they knew God, they glorified him not as God, neither were thankful; but became vain in their imaginations, and their foolish heart was darkened."* (Romans 1:21) As their hardened hearts further influenced their actions, these pre-flood men committed greater sin. *"For out of the heart proceed evil thoughts, murders, adulteries, fornications, thefts, false witness, blasphemies..."* (Matthew 15:19) In the days of Noah, men had so defiled themselves that evil works were their constant meditation. *"And GOD*

Good and Evil, No Greater Joy Ministries

saw that the wickedness of man was great in the earth, and that every imagination of the thoughts of his heart was only evil continually." (Genesis 6:5)

God is very merciful, but He will not ignore sin. Some people misinterpret God's forbearance as indifference. The Bible says of the wicked, *"They slay the widow and the stranger, and murder the fatherless. Yet they say, The LORD shall not see, neither shall the God of Jacob regard it."* (Psalm 94:6-7) To such as these, God gives a severe warning: *"When thou sawest a thief, then thou con-*

sentedst with him, and hast been partaker with adulterers. Thou givest thy mouth to evil, and thy tongue frameth deceit. Thou sittest and speakest against thy brother; thou slanderest thine own mother's son. These things hast thou done, and I kept silence; thou thoughtest that I was altogether such an one as thyself: but I will reprove thee, and set them in order before thine eyes. Now consider this, ye that forget God, lest I tear you in pieces, and there be none to deliver." (Psalm 50:18-22)

The people of Noah's day completely disregarded God. Finally, the Lord purposed to judge men for their evil and utterly destroy them from the face of the earth. *"And it repented the LORD that he had made man on the earth, and it grieved him at his heart. And the LORD said, I will destroy man whom I have created from the face of the earth; both man, and beast, and the creeping thing, and the fowls of the air; for it repenteth me that I have made them."* (Genesis 6:6-7)

God's Covenant with Noah

Despite the wickedness spreading throughout the world, one man and his family still honored God. That man's name was Noah. He was not without sin, but he was nonetheless known as a just man. The Bible says in Genesis 6:8, *"But Noah found grace in the eyes of the Lord."*

Because Noah followed the Lord and believed His word, God showed grace, delivering him and his family from the coming judgment. He said to Noah in Genesis 6:17-18, *"And, behold, I, even I, do bring a flood of waters upon the earth, to destroy all flesh, wherein is the breath of life, from under heaven; and every thing that is in the earth shall die. But with thee will I establish my covenant; and thou shalt come into the ark, thou, and thy sons, and thy wife, and thy sons' wives with thee."*

In Scripture, a covenant is a mutual agreement whereby two parties enter into a relationship based on trust. The covenant that God made with Noah was conditional, hinging directly on Noah's willingness to obey specific instructions which God had given him. If Noah did not honor the conditions of God's covenant, he would perish with the wicked when the day of judgment came.

Key Concept

In Scripture, a covenant is a mutual agreement whereby two parties enter into a relationship based on trust.

The Bible Says

"By faith Noah, being warned of God of things not seen as yet, moved with fear, prepared an ark to the saving of his house; by the which he condemned the world, and became heir of the righteousness which is by faith." (Hebrews 11:7)

The Ark

In preparing to bring the flood upon the earth, God gave Noah the plans for an enormous boat, called the ark, which would provide a safe haven for him and his family. It would also be the means of preserving the animals. In Genesis 6:14-16, God said to Noah: *"Make thee an ark of gopher wood; rooms shalt thou make in the ark, and shalt pitch it within and without with pitch. And this*

is the fashion which thou shalt make it of: The length of the ark shall be three hundred cubits, the breadth of it fifty cubits, and the height of it thirty cubits. A window shalt thou make to the ark, and in a cubit shalt thou finish it above; and the door of the ark shalt thou set in the side thereof; with lower, second, and third stories shalt thou make it."

No one knows how long Noah worked on building the ark, but by comparing his age at the close of chapter five (500 years old) with his age at the time of the ark's completion (600 years old) it would seem that it took about 100 years. During this time, Noah knew that his friends and neighbors would be doomed if they did not join him in the ark. As he worked, Noah did his best to warn them to flee from God's imminent judgment. *"And [God] spared not the old world, but saved Noah the eighth person, a <u>preacher of righteousness</u>..."* (2 Peter 2:5)

Meanwhile, God waited for the completion of the ark. All was quiet, but Noah knew very well that one day soon, God's wrath would come. By then it would be too late.

The Bible Says

"And [God] spared not the old world, but saved Noah the eighth person, a preacher of righteousness, bringing in the flood upon the world of the ungodly." (2 Peter 2:5)

Did you know?

The civilization in Noah's day was likely quite advanced. The protracted life-span of men, a common language, fewer negative effects from environment, and the slower aging process would all have contributed to great scientific and technological development. Noah would have had all the necessary resources and laborers for building one of the largest wooden boats ever made. This is exactly what he did.

How big was the ark, really? The cubit, a unit of measure Noah used in constructing the ark, was the length of a man's forearm from elbow to fingertip. It was approximately 18 inches (46 cm), but its size could vary depending on the culture and people group. Most researchers agree that the ark was at least 450 feet (137 m) long, 75 feet (23 m) wide, and 45 feet (14 m) high.

In practical terms, 3 olympic-sized swimming pools lined up end to end would be required in order to float Noah's ark. The vessel was almost twice as long as a Boeing 747 aircraft, and was as tall as a four-story building. Not only was it large, it was extremely stable. Built at a ratio of 6 times as long as it was wide, a proportion still used for modern cargo ships, the craft would not be easily overturned. The ark was eventually exceeded in size, but not until the late 19th century when steel was introduced into shipbuilding.

Preliminary Reading – Before beginning this portion of the lesson, please read **Genesis 7** in your Bible.

The Great Flood

The people of Noah's day must have thought his warnings of a global flood quite fantastical. "You mean God is going to send a flood to kill us all? He wouldn't do that! Don't you know that God loves everyone? What a fanatic you are, Noah!" The people did not believe God's warning, but hardened their hearts against Him. *"Behold, these are the ungodly, Who prosper in the world; they increase in riches. … Surely thou didst set them in slippery places: Thou castedst them down into destruction. How are they brought into desolation, as in a moment! They are utterly consumed with terrors." (Psalm 73:12, 18–19)*

Despite the mocking of those around him, Noah followed God's instructions implicitly. When the ark was finished, God spoke again to Noah: *"…Come thou and all thy house into the ark; for thee have I seen righteous before me in this generation. … For yet seven days, and I will cause it to rain upon the earth forty days and forty nights; and every living substance that I have made will I destroy from off the face of the earth." (Genesis 7:1, 4)*

For the next seven days, Noah and his family worked to load all they would need into the ark. As they made preparations, something supernatural occurred. Animals from every corner of the earth came to the ark of their own accord, compelled by the very hand of God. *"And [the animals] went in unto Noah into the ark, two and two of all flesh, wherein is the breath of life. And they that went in, went in male and female of all flesh, as God had commanded him: and the LORD shut him in." (Genesis 7:15-16)*

Good and Evil, No Greater Joy Ministries

Good and Evil, No Greater Joy Ministries

Finally, God's terrible wrath was unleashed on the earth, resulting in the biggest cataclysm that our planet has ever seen. *"In the six hundredth year of Noah's life, in the second month, the seventeenth day of the month, the same day were all the fountains of the great deep broken up, and the windows of heaven were opened. And the rain was upon the earth forty days and forty nights… And all flesh died that moved upon the earth, both of fowl, and of cattle, and of beast, and of every creeping thing that creepeth upon the earth, and every man: All in whose nostrils was the breath of life, of all that was in the dry land, died. And every living substance was destroyed which was upon the face of the ground, both man, and cattle, and the creeping things, and the fowl of the heaven; and they were destroyed from the earth: and Noah only remained alive, and they that were with him in the ark." (Genesis 7:11-12, 21-23)*

For years, mankind completely ignored God. They disobeyed Him, rebelled against Him, and forgot Him. They not only hated their own Creator, but they hated one another. When dawn broke on that terrible day of judgment, the earth was filled with people. But by nightfall, only eight were left alive.

Good and Evil, No Greater Joy Ministries

The Bible Says

"For the wages of sin is death..." (Romans 6:23)

The Bible Says

"For evildoers shall be cut off: But those that wait upon the Lord, they shall inherit the earth. For yet a little while, and the wicked shall not be: Yea, thou shalt diligently consider his place, and it shall not be." (Psalm 37:9–10)

Did you know?

How did Noah fit all the animals in the ark? Scientists who have calculated the number of pairs of clean and unclean animals generally agree that there would have been approximately 16,000 animals on board. Only a small percentage of those would have been larger than an average sheep. A train of 45[1] boxcars could easily carry all the animals. But the volume of the ark was equal to approximately 1.52 million cubic feet, the equivalent of 288 boxcars! This was more than enough room to house the animals, food and water, and Noah's family.

---

1. assuming a length of 50 feet per boxcar

Preliminary Reading – Before beginning this portion of the lesson, please read **Genesis 8** in your Bible.

The Timeline of the Flood

Genesis 8 presents an exact timeline which describes the progression and conclusion of the flood. Specific dates and lengths of time are given for each stage. A close look at the events of the flood shows that the Bible always defines its own terminology. One could wonder as to the time spans mentioned in the flood passage. For example, when the Bible says "the tenth month", as it does in Genesis 8:5, to which month is it referring? How many days does the month contain? Most nations today use the Gregorian calendar, which has 365 days in a year (366 in leap years). The months in the Gregorian calendar can be as short as 28 days or as long as 31. However, this method of tracking time was not introduced until the year 1582, so it cannot be assumed that a month in Noah's time was reckoned in the same way.

The Bible not only gives exact dates and times, but it never leaves the reader to guess as to the meaning of chronological terms. A careful reading of Genesis 7 and 8 reveals that God specifically defines the terms "year" and "month". Consider Genesis 7:11: *"In the six hundredth year of Noah's life, in the second month, the seventeenth day of the month, the same day were all the fountains of the great deep broken up, and the windows of heaven were opened."* In this verse, God marks the start of a new year, calling it the 600th year of Noah's life. Using Noah's birthday month as a starting point, He states that the flood occurred in the second month from that time. Thus, the second month was not February, but rather the second month of the 600th year in Noah's life.

In the same way, when the passage speaks of "the tenth month", it is referring to the tenth month in that year of his life.

But how many days should be ascribed to a month? According to Genesis 7:11, the first day of the flood was 600-02-17 (using the date format YEAR-MONTH-DAY as shown in Genesis 7:11). In Genesis 8:4 another exact date is given: the day the ark rested. *"And the ark rested in the seventh month, on the seventeenth day of the month, upon the mountains of Ararat."* Clearly, the flood began on 600-02-17, and that the waters went down enough for the ark to rest on 600-07-17, a time span of exactly five months.

However, before the Scripture mentions the ark coming to rest, it first reveals another time increment pertinent to determining the length of a month.

- *"And the waters prevailed upon the earth an hundred and fifty days."* (Genesis 7:24)
- *"And the waters returned from off the earth continually: and after the end of the hundred and fifty days the waters were abated."* (Genesis 8:3)

Immediately after this second mention of the 150 days, we are told that the ark rested on 600-07-17. This provides two important facts:

- The time from the beginning of rain fall to the day when the ark rested was five months.
- The time from the beginning of rain fall to the day when the waters no longer prevailed, but were abated enough for the ark to rest, was 150 days.

The passage indicates that the two time periods are synonymous. Taking the 150 days and dividing it by 5 months gives the length of one month: exactly 30 days.

150 days = 5 months (Genesis 8:3-4)

150 days ÷ 5 months = 30 days per month

Timeline of the Great Flood

Basis of reckoning: Noah's life (beginning with the year 600)
Format: YEAR-MONTH-DAY (e.g. 600-02-17)

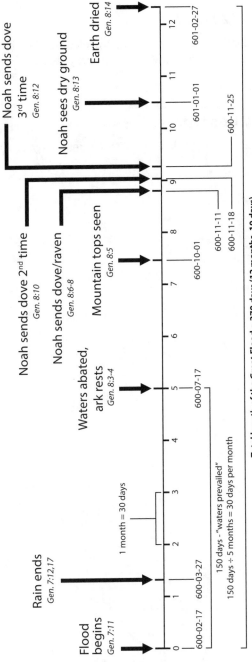

Key Concept

The Bible is a divine story unparalleled by any other document, exact in its history and bold in its prophecy.

Key Concept

The Bible always defines its own terminology.

God Delivers Noah and His Family

The rains which God brought upon the earth continued without ceasing for forty days. The earth was completely covered with water. Even the peaks of the highest mountains were nearly 23 feet (7 m) under the surface! (See Genesis 7:20) During this time, Noah may have been tempted to doubt God's faithfulness. How much longer would they have to stay on the ark? Would their food and supplies last? But God did not forget about Noah.

"And God remembered Noah, and every living thing, and all the cattle that was with him in the ark: and God made a wind to pass over the earth, and the waters asswaged; The fountains also of the deep and the windows of heaven were stopped, and the rain from heaven was restrained;" (Genesis 8:1-2)

With the waters already in recession, the ark came to rest five months to the day after the flood began. At that time, God directed the ark to just the right place of safety atop the peaks of a mountain range called Ararat. From this vantage point, Noah and his family eagerly looked for any sight of land. Nearly three months later, mountain tops finally appeared above the surface of the water. Waiting yet another 40 days, Noah sent out two birds, a raven and a dove. Finding no available place to land, the dove soon returned to the ark. Seven days later, Noah sent the dove out again. This time, it returned with a leaf from an olive tree, evidence that land had indeed appeared. The third time the dove was sent out, it did not return.

Finally, the time came when God commanded Noah and his family to leave the ark. After 370 days in the ark, they were able to walk once again on dry ground. God had promised them salvation and had fulfilled His word.

The earth was now a very different place than they had known prior to the flood. Everything that mankind had built and accomplished up to that point had been destroyed: roads, farms, cities, and governments. All that Noah and his family possessed was what they had taken with them into the ark. And yet they were alive. In spite of the hardships facing them, they were grateful to the Lord that He had spared them from perishing with the wicked. Truly He had shown Himself to be a God of mercy!

The first thing Noah did after leaving the ark was to build an altar and worship the Lord. *"And Noah builded an altar unto the LORD; and took of every clean beast, and of every clean fowl, and offered burnt offerings on the altar."* (Genesis 8:20) God was pleased with Noah's offering, as He had been with Abel's. *"And the LORD smelled a sweet savour; and the LORD said in his heart, I will not again curse the ground any more for man's sake; for the imagination of man's heart is evil from his youth; neither will I again smite any more every thing living, as I have done. While the earth remaineth, seedtime and harvest, and cold and heat, and summer and winter, and day and night shall not cease."* (Genesis 8:21-22)

Key Concept

Noah was not without sin, but because he believed God, God showed him grace.

Preliminary Reading – Before beginning this portion of the lesson, please read **Genesis 9-10** in your Bible.

A New Civilization

Noah's exit from the ark was not only the start of a new life for him and his family, it was the beginning of a new civilization. Much as Adam was made king over the earth after Creation, so Noah was given dominion after the flood. All other men who had once enjoyed positions of power were now dead because of their sin, and God Himself placed Noah at the head of the human race.

God gave to Noah and his descendants specific commandments which would govern their conduct on the earth.

- COMMANDMENT #1: Replenish the earth. *"And God blessed Noah and his sons, and said unto them, Be fruitful, and multiply, and replenish the earth."* *(Genesis 9:1)* Because there were only eight people on the entire planet at this time, God desired that they would bear children and repopulate the earth.

- COMMANDMENT #2: The meat of animals may be eaten, but not the blood. *"Every moving thing that liveth shall be meat for you; even as the green herb have I given you all things. But flesh with the life thereof, which is the blood thereof, shall ye not eat."* *(Genesis 9:3-4)* The Lord regards blood as sacred because it contains the life of the body. Furthermore, blood is the only substance which can atone for sin. (See Leviticus 17:11) In both the Old and New Testaments, the Bible explicitly forbids eating blood. (See Deuteronomy 12:23, Acts 15:20)

- COMMANDMENT #3: Do not kill. *"And surely your blood of your lives will I require; at the hand of every beast will I require it, and at the hand of man; at the hand of every man's brother will I require the life of man. Whoso sheddeth man's blood, by man shall his blood be shed: for in the image of God made he man." (Genesis 9:5-6)* One of the great sins which brought down God's judgment on the pre-flood world was that of violence. (See Genesis 6:11) As the new world began, God made it very clear to Noah that murder was to be punished with death.

After giving these commands, God reiterated His covenant with mankind, promising never again to destroy the world with a flood of water. All covenants in Scripture are accompanied by a token or sign, to be a reminder of the covenant to both parties. God's sign to assure men that He would never again cause a global flood was one of the most beautiful phenomena in nature: the rainbow. Thousands of years later, the rainbow continues to serve as a breathtaking reminder of God's goodness towards His creation.

Key Concept

Whenever God establishes a covenant with men, He always gives a token or sign.

Did you know?

The story of the Flood has not only been preserved in the Bible, but also in folklore. Hundreds of cultures all throughout the world contain legends of a great deluge. These stories are often distorted after centuries of being told and retold, but they nonetheless contain several common themes:

- Mankind had become very sinful.
- A higher power destroyed the world by a flood.
- A small group of people was saved in a boat.

> Preliminary Reading – Before beginning this portion of the lesson, please read **Genesis 11** in your Bible.

The Tower of Babel

As men increased on the earth, they made the same error as their predecessors: they forgot God and His commandments. Specifically, God had instructed men to replenish the whole earth. This would have meant spreading out to inhabit various regions, but Noah's descendants instead congregated in a single geographical area. At this time, they all spoke the same language. *"And the whole earth was of one language, and of one speech."* *(Genesis 11:1)* Finding a large plain called Shinar, they decided to build a city, and also began construction on a great tower. The Bible states that the Lord came down to see what these men were doing, and it displeased Him.

Perhaps men did not believe God's promise to never again send a global flood. They may have doubted His word, aspiring to build a tower high enough to withstand any flood and strong enough to provide them protection. However, the problem was not the tower itself, but men's desire to exalt themselves to heaven. Whatever their motivation, clearly mankind had started down the same path that Satan himself once took. *"...I will ascend into heaven, I will exalt my throne above the stars of God: I will sit also upon the mount of the congregation, in the sides of the north: I will ascend above the heights of the clouds; I will be like the most High."* *(Isaiah 14:13–14)*

God stopped the work of these men very effectively: He confused their speech. The vital importance of language in uniting people is easily recognized. If a group of people does not share a common language, their potential to accomplish anything useful is extremely limited. In contrast, God acknowledged that Noah's descendants could achieve whatever they set their minds to, on account of having a universal language. *"And the Lord said, Behold, the people is one, and they have all one language; and this they begin to do: and now nothing will be restrained from them, which they have imagined to do. Go to, let us go down, and there confound their language, that they may not understand one another's speech. So the Lord scattered them abroad from thence upon the face of all the earth: and they left off to build the city."* (Genesis 11:6–8)

The Hebrew word "Babel" means confusion. The confusion at the tower of Babel gave rise to the diverse nations and language groups that exist on the earth. Even today, cooperation between language groups is impossible unless the communication barrier can be overcome.

The Bible Says

"For whosoever exalteth himself shall be abased; and he that humbleth himself shall be exalted." (Luke 14:11)

Did you know?

Archeologists have discovered the remains of numerous towers, called ziggurats, built by ancient civilizations in Iran and Iraq. Ziggurats were built in receding tiers upon a rectangular, oval, or square platform with an ascending staircase that ended in a temple on the top. The Tower of Babel is generally considered to have been built after this fashion.

Conclusion

The account of Noah and the Great Flood is one of the most amazing in the Bible. Aside from the sheer awe inspired by the story, there is also an important parallel. Just as God showed grace to Noah and provided a way for him to be saved from the flood, so He has shown grace to us through His Son, the Lord Jesus Christ. *"For by grace are ye saved through faith; and that not of yourselves: it is the gift of God: Not of works, lest any man should boast."* *(Ephesians 2:8-9)*

From what do we need to be saved? The Scriptures plainly declare that there is coming another day of judgment, similar in many ways to the flood that destroyed the world in Noah's time. But this judgment will not be one of water. The next time God judges the world, it will be by fire. (See 2 Peter 3:10) Additionally, every individual will stand before God and give account for the deeds he has committed. John the Baptist spoke of God's judgment to the Pharisees in Matthew 3:7 when he said, *"O generation of vipers, who hath warned you to flee from the wrath to come?"* Paul the Apostle also describes this judgment, warning the sinner: *"But after thy hardness and impenitent heart treasurest up unto thyself wrath against the day of wrath and revelation of the righteous judgment of God;"* *(Romans 2:5)*

The Bible gives several other accounts of this judgment, but one of the most detailed is found in Revelation 20:11-15, where the Apostle John records the following: *"And I saw a great white throne, and him that sat on it, from whose face the earth and the heaven fled away; and there was found no place for them. And I saw the dead, small and great, stand before God; and the books were opened: and another book was opened, which is the book of life: and the dead were judged out of those things which were written in the books, according to their works. And the sea gave up the dead which were in it; and death and hell delivered up the dead which were in them: and they were judged every man according to their works. And death and hell were cast into the lake of fire. This is the second death. And whosoever was not found written in the book of life was cast into the lake of fire."*

Since all have sinned, how can anyone hope to be delivered from this condemnation? Just as God provided a safe place of salvation for Noah, so He has provided such a place for us: the Lord Jesus Christ. Consider the following:

- *"For as in Adam all die, even so <u>in Christ</u> shall all be made alive." (1 Corinthians 15:22)*

- *"There is therefore now no condemnation to them which are <u>in Christ Jesus</u>…" (Romans 8:1)*

- *"But God commendeth his love toward us, in that, while we were yet sinners, Christ died for us. Much more then, being now justified by his blood, we shall be saved from wrath <u>through [Christ]</u>." (Romans 5:8-9)*

- *"For the wages of sin is death; but the gift of God is eternal life <u>through Jesus Christ</u> our Lord." (Romans 6:23)*

Today's popular opinion suggests that there are many ways to be saved. Consider what would have happened to Noah if he had said, "I really don't need this ark. I've proven myself to be a good person, I'm religious and I certainly believe in God. I'm sure everything will be OK." If Noah had not built the ark, he would never have survived the flood. The ark was the only refuge during the flood, and anyone who was not inside perished.

On the other hand, what if one of Noah's sinful neighbors had repented and decided to join Noah in the ark. Suppose he had said, "I've been wicked all my life. I've hated God and done wrong to other people. But I fear God's judgment and I believe that Noah is telling the truth about this coming flood. I will join him in the ark." That man would have been saved. Why? Because he believed God and entered the ark.

Jesus Christ is the only way of salvation given to men. It matters not how much we know, how good we are in comparison to someone else, or how much we try to impress God with our works. If we are not <u>in Christ</u>, we will be condemned to the lake of fire on Judgment Day. How do we come into Christ? We simply believe on His name. That is, we trust fully in the sacrifice that He made for us on the cross.

The Apostle Peter said of Jesus Christ, *"Neither is there salvation in any other: for there is none other name under heaven given among men, whereby we must be saved." (Acts 4:12)*

Jesus Himself said in John 11:25-26: *"...I am the resurrection, and the life: he that believeth in me, though he were dead, yet shall he live: And whosoever liveth and believeth in me shall never die. Believest thou this?"*

Key Concept

Jesus Christ is our "safe place" of salvation.

Notes

_____

_____

_____

_____

_____

_____

_____

_____

_____

_____

_____

_____

_____

_____

_____

_____

_____

_____

_____

_____

_____

_____

_____

_____

_____

_____

_____

_____

_____

Notes

_____

_____

_____

_____

_____

_____

_____

_____

_____

_____

_____

_____

_____

_____

_____

_____

_____

_____

_____

_____

_____

_____

_____

_____

_____

_____

Before continuing, please answer all the questions provided in the Q&A Booklet for this lesson. If you do not have a Q&A Booklet for this lesson, please contact your coach.

GOOD AND EVIL INTERNATIONAL

IN OUR VISION, THE GOOD GUYS WIN.

Good and Evil International forms the base of operations for a unique set of warriors for Christ. We are a Bible-based, missions-focused organization that delivers the saving message of the Gospel of Christ through innovative, technologically savvy media.

Good and Evil International produces and distributes print, electronic, and video versions of the Good and Evil graphic Bible storybook and other communication products. We offer ways for supporters to actively participate in mission opportunities. We have sent over 100,000 books to prisons worldwide; though this outreach, many have come to know the Lord.

"My children just love this Bible in animation form! They will pour over it for hours and act out scenes from different books."

– TARA

"We bought 2 of these. One for our kids and another for a friend's kids...we LOVE this book!"

–JANEL